MW00628191

The
Drinking
NANNY

The Drinking NANNY

CODES TO LIVE BY WHEN THE KIDS DRIVE YOU TO DRINK

KIMBERLY JOAN

BOOKLOGIX·
Alpharetta, GA

The anecdotes described in this book are for entertainment purposes. They are reflective of the author's personal experiences and are not intended to be diagnostic or prescriptive of behavioral issues. You are encouraged to consult with a pediatric medical or behavioral specialist as necessary. Names and identifying details have been changed to protect the privacy of individuals.

Copyright © 2019 by Kimberly Joan

All rights reserved. No part of this book may be reproduced or transmitted in any form or by any means, electronic or mechanical, including photocopying, recording, or any information storage and retrieval system, without permission in writing from the publisher. For more information, address BookLogix, c/o Permissions Department, 1264 Old Alpharetta Rd., Alpharetta, GA 30005.

ISBN: 978-1-61005-960-2 - Paperback
eISBN: 978-1-61005-961-9 - ePub
eISBN: 978-1-61005-962-6 - mobi

Library of Congress Control Number: 2019901964

Printed in the United States of America   0 2 1 3 1 9

LEGO® is a registered trademark of The LEGO Group. Used with permission.

⊛This paper meets the requirements of ANSI/NISO Z39.48-1992 (Permanence of Paper)

Illustrations by Scott Mattson
Special thanks to Denise Renee

This book is dedicated to all the families that allowed me into their homes to witness their love and sacrifice of being a parent.

To my mom and dad, two educators who raised and taught me everything about love, discipline, and laughter.

To Jeff and Trish—you already know, main! LOL! Love you guys!

To Truck—we have come so far, and the best is yet to come!

To my dear sweet Keith—I prayed for you, and I am grateful for God's answer.

$\mathcal{C}$ontents

Introduction

All about the Drinking Nanny

Hi, I'm Kimberly. "My kids" call me Key, Ms. Kimberly, or MeMi, but you can call me the Drinking Nanny.

Now, I know what you're thinking! But before you have a Code 57/11 on me (pronounced "fiddy-seben eleven" in a Southern accent), I need you to bring it down to at least a Code 12 or 13. This isn't anything to freak out over! I don't drink around kids or while I am on the job. As a parent, you know before the day is over that your kids may "drive you to drink" at least one good time! I say, once the little ones finally lay down (and stay down), you will be ready for an adult sippy cup full of an after-hours drink.

That's what I mean!

When I'm not working, I enjoy drinking. My adult beverage of choice is light beer. What's your go-to drink when the kids make you want to sip on something strong? No worries if you don't have one. At the end of each chapter, once you've learned how I handle challenging behavior, I'll recommend a drink to help you wind down from the whining!

Here's one thing to know about me: I love having fun, and I enjoy making people laugh! Just remember, I'm telling you now so you won't take offense to my off-the-wall comments; just chuckle and roll with it.

So, let's get into it. I'll start this book off by answering the obvious questions: Who am I? What is this book about? And why did I write it?

Who Is the Drinking Nanny?

I am single with no kids of my own, but I know I was born to work with children.

Growing up in Arkansas, I started a babysitting hustle as a preteen. I used to take care of the eight-and-under group during choir rehearsal at church for six bucks per kid. Fifty or more dollars in less than two hours? Boy, I was a shark at ten years old!

Throughout middle and high school, I was the preferred babysitter in my area. My mom, a teacher, encouraged my ingenuity. She shuttled me to my gigs until I could drive myself. My dad, rest his soul, was an educator, too. He was always proud of my hustle.

My business venture went on hiatus when I took six years to finish college. Why the extra two years? Because college wasn't 100 percent compatible with my self-diagnosed "focus issues!" If partying had been a major, I was headed for a double degree in it. The reality was, I changed my major every time I got bored. Ultimately, I was "scared straight" into finishing my bachelor's degree in history—but you'd need to spring for a six-pack with me if you wanted to hear that story!

In my early twenties, I got stuck in Atlanta after one crazy weekend of partying. (Two lemon-drop shots could coax me into telling that tale!) I had no money to get home to Arkansas. When I called my parents, they told me that I would know what to do and to come up with a plan. So, I resorted to what I knew: I got a job at a daycare center to raise the money I needed to get back home. But here is the funny thing: after I earned the cash, I never left Atlanta. I had found my way to what I loved—making a living caring for children.

It wasn't long before my side-hustling skills kicked in again. The daycare parents asked me to babysit for them, as they always needed an extra hand during the evenings and on weekends. Things went well for a while. Then, I got restless. Although I liked working at the daycare and babysitting on the side, I felt I was working too hard for too little money. When I learned I could make more money as a private nanny, I set out to do so.

I quit working for daycare centers and signed up for nanny agencies. I requested to receive assignments only in Buckhead, a wealthy section of Atlanta. Then, I enacted a plan that landed me private clients. In less than a year of discovering the field, I was steadily working in the homes of people willing to pay top dollar for me to care for their children.

Over the last fifteen years, I've worked as a nanny for well-known sports and entertainment figures, media moguls, and famous business leaders. It has come with cool perks. I've conversed with Hollywood royalty and even stayed at Baker's Bay Island. Oh, the stories I could tell and the "tea" I could spill . . . allegedly! But, those tales are for another day (or possibly another book—written anonymously, of course!).

What This Book Is About

My intent with this book is to help parents, grandparents, aunts, uncles—*anyone* who cares for children. I don't consider myself a childcare expert, but I've literally cared for hundreds of children, while most people only raise a few. I've learned a thing or two along the way.

I've been in the kid-raising game a long time. Not one kid has ever come with an instruction manual! I mean, you are blessed with this tiny little life that is placed in your arms at the hospital, then shoved out the door with the insane task of keeping it alive for eighteen years! Then, you've got to be sure to cram enough information into them so they can keep themselves alive for the next sixty-five or so years beyond that!

With hundreds of ways to approach raising a child, how do you know if (and when) you are doing something right as a parent? It's never-ending, on-the-job training. Kids behave perfectly when they are sleeping; it's when they're awake and working your last nerve (which was hanging by a thread) that you could use help!

No one ever tells you what to do when you're in the middle of Walmart and little Bobby launches a full-on tantrum and either super glues himself to the floor or looks like the lead break dancer in Thriller! I mean, is there a guidebook for that?

Actually, there is. You're holding it!

How to Survive Tantrums, Sibling Wars, and "What the %*#@ was THAT?"

See, I have a unique perspective on raising children. I am essentially a stranger who goes into people's homes as a new authority figure to the kids. So, when I see challenging behavior from the kids, it's imperative I do something different that genuinely captures the little ones' attention. When children are acting out, or there is a crazy situation going on, parents' go-to responses— yelling, bargaining, and time-out threats—only add fuel to the fire.

If you've ever done that (and who hasn't?), please hear my heart: I am not trying to imply that you're a terrible parent. Frankly, I believe anyone willing to sacrifice their time and money to raise a kid is automatically a good parent! After all, not everyone sticks around to take care of the life they created. By virtue of reading these words, you're awesome in my mind because you care enough to find more effective parenting techniques than the ones perhaps used to raise you. But, I also understand falling back on habitual behavior. I can relate to having long and challenging days at work. When you get home, you just want to relax and enjoy your family. It only takes one tiny moment for the kids to confirm that peace will not be on the evening agenda. All the yoga and meditation in the world can't get you zen at that moment!

But you know what can? Laughter!

See, I've found that during tense moments, laughter can break up the atmosphere and give you a different perspective. Laughter can make a situation easier to resolve. When you think about it, many of the things kids do *are* rather funny. It just doesn't feel funny at the time. So, I've come up with a way to help ease tense moments and inject humor and fun into disciplining. At the very least, you will certainly laugh as you make your way through this book and look at your children's behaviors in a different light. As a result, your kids will act right and you can stay in your right mind. Best of all, you will have permission to pour yourself a stiff one once you've survived what feels like an endless reign of terror. It's a win-win!

So, how do I make dealing with kids seem like a walk on a sundrenched beach with a Mai Tai? It's all about the Codes!

Mayday! We're Having a Code 12!

I encounter situations everyday that I've classified into Codes, or a system to describe different kids' behaviors. Each Code has my recommended solutions for neutralizing the situation at hand. I always teach my Codes to my kids (I call all the children I take care of "my kids," by the way!). When they are exhibiting the wrong behavior, I can calmly call out the Code, and they understand what they should do to correct themselves.

What inspired the Codes? I got the idea from airports and my favorite medical shows. Every time I fly, they say over the intercom: "The airport is on code orange today." On TV medical dramas, they often say, "Code blue, code blue! I need a crash cart!" When a team hears the Code, they immediately understand what's happening. They can spring into action with the proper response. So I thought, *Why don't I create Codes for my kids?* Codes help you quickly identify a situation and the protocol for handling it.

Trust me, you'll come to appreciate my Codes. When little Suzie is having a Code 13 or is in the middle of a fiddy-seben eleven, my recommended drinks at the end of each section in this book will be your "crash cart." Why? Because you'll need something to resuscitate you!

Kids exhibit the same problematic behaviors and get into similar scenarios every day. I have a standardized way to deal with each one. When I say to one of my kids, "You're having a Code 12," it helps them "stop, drop, and-roll," meaning it gives them the space to pause, think, and correct their own behavior before consequences are enacted.

I used numbers for the Codes to help my younger ones practice their counting. Once a child knows my Codes and understands what I expect of them, I don't have to intervene all the time. One thing each Code has in common is that I don't encourage, feed into, or engage with unacceptable behavior, because that always escalates the situation.

The Codes are a friendly way to discipline. For instance, say two sisters are playing with dolls, but they start fighting. I could respond with a typical approach by yelling, "Stop taking your sister's doll! If you two don't stop fighting, I will send you both to time-out!" However, matching their aggression and anger with my own only fuels the negativity. So, I can usually nip a situation like this in the bud with a simple question: "Girls, do we have a Code 17 here? Do we need a time-out?"

They'll pause and think about the consequence for a moment. The frustration will drain from their faces. Their voices will drop. They'll lower their heads and mumble, "No, MeMi. We'll share." Then they'll pout and play together again. Peace may last for the rest of the day or only ten minutes, but if they start bickering again, I repeat the process until they finally share or stop playing altogether.

Now, don't call me a parenting coach, kid whisperer, an expert, or Super Nanny. I'm just sharing with you what I know works from my personal experience. I've been teaching these Codes to my kids over the years, and they learn quickly. My parents? Bless y'all's hearts, not so much! You guys try to learn them, but in the middle of a hectic situation I've heard some of you shout, "We have a Code 8! What Code is it? A Code 39! Uh, a Code . . . We've got a Code!"

My parents make my sides hurt from laughing with that one!

Ultimately, you are holding this book because I want to teach you my Codes. I want you to get to your adult sippy cup at the end of your day with ease. Are you ready? Here we go!

Wait, wait, WAIT!

I have to give you a quick disclaimer. I will share real stories and actual situations I have encountered while working for various families to help illustrate my Codes. All names are anonymized. I changed and/or fictionalized some details to protect all my employers' privacy. Why? Because if this book doesn't make me a millionaire right away, I will still need a job!

Okay, now we can rock and roll! First stop, Code 11.

Chapter 1

Code 11: Preparation for the Destination

Have you ever heard the term "gateway drug"? Here is the concept: If someone, particularly a teenager, begins exhibiting negative behaviors such as drinking or smoking cigarettes, it increases the likelihood they will eventually use illegal drugs. Well, think of Code 11 as a gateway drug. It is very much a "gateway Code," and not just because it's the first one I'm giving you.

Parents, this is not a drill! Only YOU can prevent a Code 11 from happening! A Code 11 is when kids go stir-crazy from boredom on car rides, sitting in waiting rooms, etc. That's why it is so important to pack all necessary toys, pacifiers, art supplies, electronics, etc. to last the duration of every planned trip or outing. The best way to handle a Code 11 is to not let it happen. How? Every time you get ready to step out of the door with your kids, be prepared to keep the kids happily occupied for the duration of your trip. Trust me, it's for your own sanity.

Before you're tempted to think packing tools kids need for an outing is not a big deal, pause for a moment. I'm sure you can think of a few times when you've left the house without the tools necessary to arrive at the destination and back home with your last nerve still intact. Being prepared for the time it takes to get to your destination keeps the kids happy. In turn, they will stay out of your hair. They're not crying, complaining, fighting each other, or otherwise harassing us adults.

The biggest mistake you can make is to think: *Well, we're just running to the store,* or, *We're just going to the park. They'll be fine once they get there.*

WRONG!

Did I mention that Code 11 is like a gateway drug for kids? See, the real issue with Code 11 is, it can transition into the next code, meaning it can very easily turn into a Code 12 (tantrum), which we will discuss in the next chapter. Let me show you what I mean. One evening, one of my parents whose children ranged from three to seven made a last-minute decision. "Let's go out to dinner with the kids," Mom announced.

We quickly mobilized and packed up a three-year-old, a five-year-old, a seven-year-old, and his friend into their SUV. Mom took nothing to keep the kids occupied. When I suggested it, she said, "Why do we need all those things? We're *just* going to dinner. They will be eating. They'll be occupied."

That "just" word will get you in trouble every time! Never forget that a few minutes feels like an eternity to a child. And when they are not occupied during that eternity, it's a living hell to them. Have you heard the phrase "misery loves company"? Very soon, bored kids make sure you experience their personal hell along with them!

Now, let's get back to our Code 11 already in progress . . .

We got to our local Japanese restaurant, and I'm sure you can imagine how restless the kids were at this point. The kids fidgeted as they waited for the food with nothing to do. Mom constantly scolded the two youngest ones, "Sit still! Our food will be here soon."

You know that didn't work, right?

It took a few minutes to sink in, but the three-year-old realized that his Lovie, his favorite comfort toy, wasn't with him. (Small kids always have that one toy or object they can't live without. As long as it is in their possession, all is right in their world.) He cried, inconsolable because he wanted to go home to get Lovie.

Without a doll or paper and crayons, the five-year-old got interested in stuff on the floor, harassing mom, and picking a fight with her younger brother. She did everything but sit still at the table! She practically bounced off the walls, moving from object to person and back again.

The seven-year-old and his friend thought the hats the chefs were wearing looked like "ninja hats." So, they decided that they would be ninjas, too. They picked up the silverware and started sword fighting in their seats. Soon, the seats couldn't contain the butter-knife play. They roughhoused around the table. Occasionally they bumped into their sister, and that started a war of the sibling clans!

By this point, Mom was feeling embarrassed with the kids' behavior, not to mention frustrated. We were both busy trying to put out fires with the kids. Ironically, it was a real fire that finally got them all to settle down. If you've never been to a hibachi-style restaurant, the presentation can be rather dramatic. When the chef lit the fire on the grill and the flames flared up, it scared the kids, and they let out a collective yell! But, once they got over the shock, they settled down. Watching the food preparation captivated them. Fortunately, it kept their interest until the food was ready to eat.

In hindsight, this was a hilarious scene. But, as it was happening, it was a nightmare. If I had my backpack, the Code 11 could have been avoided. My backpack is famous with my kids because it is always loaded with goodies they love. I never leave home without it. It has several compartments, perfect for when I am working with a family with multiple siblings. Everyone gets their own section. I fill it with their favorite toys, activities, and snacks so I can head their meltdowns off at the pass. Even if we are on our way to or from a fun event, I prepare to keep them engaged in a constructive activity. I also make sure they never need to say "I'm hungry" or "I'm thirsty." It is how I guarantee I'll return from the destination with my sanity intact.

In my observation, parents' ideas of preparation run the gamut. Most first-time parents think they need to bring the entire house. Experienced parents just grab their tumbler of coffee, maybe a snack for the kids, and assume the little ones will amuse themselves along the way.

So, how do I recommend you prepare for your destination and avoid a Code 11–related meltdown? I've discovered that when dealing with children aged five and under, there are five must-haves you need to keep on hand to nip a Code 11 in the bud.

1. You need a full sippy cup and an extra bottle of their preferred liquid to refresh the sippy cup as necessary.

2. You need their "peeps" (short for "people") they like to roll with. Everywhere they go, they must have their bunny, fluffy, bear, unicorn, pacifier, blanket, or whatever their favorite soothing object is. You know they can't survive without it, so just bring it with you. Save your attempts at weening them off the object for the comfort of your home. Never try to ween them on the road.

3. Always keep wet wipes, paper towels, or dry burp cloths on hand.
4. Always have diapers and a change of clothes for children aged four and under.
5. Be prepared with two or three of their favorite small toys or an engaging activity so they have options for keeping themselves occupied.

Preparation for the destination is necessary for older kids, too. Nowadays, electronics like an iPad or a smartphone with games keep them pacified. For more studious or crafty kids, let them bring along an activity book or a book to read. With the kids adequately occupied, you will be free from sullen sighs, an annoying barrage of questions, or sibling fights. No more swatting kids in the back seat with your right hand while your left hand tries to keep the car straight!

Want an example of a smooth Code 11?

One time, I accompanied one of my families to a Disney on Ice show. The family had small children and a preteen. Preteens think they are too cool for school. They get bored with everything at the drop of a hat! I knew the show would mesmerize the smaller kids, but I had my backpack filled with goodies to occupy them just in case. But, my preteen concerned me the most. So, I went prepared. I had a separate, smaller bag loaded with several of her favorite activities.

About five minutes into the cheesy music and characters that delighted every toddler in the building, she rolled her eyes and looked over at me like she was just over it! Before she could even open her mouth to moan out a complaint, I tossed that smaller bag over to her. She dug in, her eyes lit up, and her demeanor changed as she pulled out something to occupy herself. I didn't hear a peep out of her for the rest of the show. You bet I was ready for my celebratory beer on that one! But, I was on the clock, so it had to wait.

To become a rock star at Code 11, be sure to bring things your kids genuinely enjoy. Let them pick out small toys and activities in advance to bring along. That way, you know they'll be engaged and stay out of your hair. Round out your pack with snacks, drinks, and anything to quickly clean up messes, and you're ready to go.

The day you take your own backpack full of preparation items and successfully return home, having avoided all the fires that Code 11 sparks, you are ready for your victory dance! That evening, I give you permission to fill your adult sippy cup with some merlot. Red wine is a lovely, calming, and soothing drink. You earned it!

Chapter 2

Code 12: A Tantrum

ACode 12 is a tantrum, a sweet symphony of an emotional outburst of frustration or anger using the voice as the primary instrument. Close your eyes and imagine this with me. On second thought, open your eyes—you have to keep reading!

Picture this: it's early on a delightful spring morning. The birds are chirping. You awake to their lovely melody and say an affirmation. You're loving life, and you're ready to start your day. It's time to wake up your son, get him breakfast, then head out for work. You go into the kitchen pantry and reach for the box of cereal, your two-year-old son's favorite breakfast. But, the box is light. You peek inside—it's empty. At first, you panic. Then you think, *That's okay. He can just try something new for breakfast today. Maybe a bowl of fruit? Yeah, that's the ticket. He likes fruit.* No sweat, right?

Spoiler alert: I name this chapter "Code 12: A Tantrum" for a reason!

So, you prepare the bowl of fruit, set it on the tray of his high chair, then go to get him out of bed. You lead your little angel into the kitchen, and he pads over to his chair. He lifts his cute little hands into the air and says, "Up!", to which you comply. He knows the morning routine, so he's expecting his bowl of cereal. You strap him into his high chair, then walk away.

Because you turn your back, you don't see the horror that washes over his angelic little face at the sight of fruit on his tray. Not seeing his beloved cereal causes him to black out! Before you can complete two steps, he lets out a forceful "NO!", and you hear the hard, plastic bowl clatter onto the floor behind you.

Houston, we have a problem! Code 12! I repeat, we have a Code 12 in progress!

Now, parents, you know from experience that it doesn't take much for a kid to throw a tantrum. A minor change in their daily routine, not getting their way, or being told no can instantly derail their attitude. Kids want what they want, right now! Younger children are still working on their language-acquisition skills, so they often act out their disappointments and frustrations.

Now, although I had you imagine this scenario, I'm sure you know this story really happened. I'm sure you also know it didn't just stop with the forceful "no" and food on the floor.

The dad this really happened to walked back to the high chair and asked, "Why did you throw the fruit on the floor?"

"No fruit!" his son replied. "Cereal!"

"I'm sorry, we are out of cereal. You are having fruit for breakfast today," Dad said.

"Noooo!" And the wailing began.

"Stop crying!" Dad said with annoyance as he prepared another bowl of fruit. "Don't you want to be a big boy?" he said, attempting a softer tone to appeal to his two-year-old's sense of reason. "Big boys don't have the same thing for breakfast every day," he said as he set a new bowl on the high chair's tray.

"NOOOO! Cereal!"

The wailing became louder and stronger. The snot and tears flowed. He shoved the bowl again, but this time Dad was hip to the game. Dad grabbed the bowl before the contents could topple over to the floor. By this point, Mom had entered the kitchen. Dad gave her a frustrated look. "Can you get him to eat, please? I need to leave now or I'll be late to work."

Kid: 1

Parents: 0

I could describe how the exchange played out with Mom over the next few painful minutes, but I'll spare you the gory details. Let's just say Mom wasn't able to score for Team Parents, either. After a few more minutes of verbal volleying with her son, she left the plate of fruit in front of him to go grab some medicine for her headache from the bathroom.

Kid: 2

Parents: 0

Once Mom stepped out, I took that opportunity to slip over to the two-year-old's chair for a quick chat. As a general rule, I don't intervene when a parent is speaking with their child unless I am explicitly invited into the conversation. And, even when a Code 12 is in progress and escalating, I don't break in unless the parents ask me. But, I was alone with the toddler, so I swooped in.

He was still crying over the bowl of fruit. By this time, though, he had downgraded his loud wail to a long, drawn out, midlevel "aaahhh" punctuated with heaving. His eyes were squinty from pumping out crocodile tears.

I stopped next to his chair and said in a hushed tone, "MeMi is going to the supermarket later. What do you think I should buy for breakfast?"

Being asked what he wanted stopped his tears. He got that dreamy, Christmas Day–anticipation gleam in his eyes. See, he loved going to the supermarket because it's a vast place that has lots and lots of stuff he liked. So, that captured his attention, but understanding I wanted to listen to him caused him to talk to me. "Cereal!" he exclaimed. No surprise there.

"Is there something else you want me to buy for breakfast?" I asked. It was my sneaky way of finding out what else he liked eating.

He thought for a second, then said, "Waffles!" Then, to my surprise, he added, "Fruit!"

I responded, "Oh! Well, what fruit should MeMi buy?"

"Umm, strawberrieees!" He showed me his cute baby teeth when he exaggerated the E.

"You eat strawberries?" I asked, feigning surprise.

"Uh-hum!" he said proudly.

"Well, we have waffles in the freezer. Should I make you one right now?" I asked.

"Yeah!" he exclaimed, clapping his cute little hands.

"You know," I continued, "there's a strawberry in your bowl right there! Can you eat that strawberry for MeMi while I go make your waffle?"

"Okay, MeMi!" He swiped at his nose with the back of his hand left hand, picked up the strawberry with his snotty right hand, and ate it.

Kid: 0

Parents: 2

Imaginary announcer guy: "The Drinking Nanny swoops in and steals the two points from the kid! All the adults in the building go wild!"

That was a smooth move, getting him to eat the fruit he was refusing just a few minutes ago, right? I'll let you call me Super Nanny on that one, because he didn't even realize I was playing for Team Parents!

Mom came back into the kitchen with the aspirin in her hand, grabbed a glass, and headed to the water dispenser in the fridge. And that's when she noticed it: no more crying, *and* her son was eating the fruit! "Wait!" she said, confused. "He's not crying! And he's eating. How did you get him to eat his fruit?" Her mouth gaped open in shock.

I turned around from the toaster and shrugged my shoulders, playing it off. "I guess crying wore him out. He said he wanted a waffle for breakfast, so I'm making him one, if that's okay."

Mom snapped her jaw shut, raised her eyebrows, and looked at the aspirin in her hands. "I guess I don't need these anymore!"

Peaceful days, beware! A Code 12 can rear its ugly head any time, any place. Unlike a Code 11, you can't prepare to avoid it. But, you can navigate it and nip it in the bud successfully. When a Code 12 is in progress, you long for it to stop. I get that. But, in the heat of the moment, parents often respond in ways that keep the Code 12 going on longer than it should. Parents' typical responses are yelling, arguing back and forth, or trying to reason with the child. Those types of reactions engage the Code 12 behavior and keep its

fire burning. During a Code 12, a child is expressing their frustration unacceptably. They are bel-
ligerent and refuse to listen. While I believe every
child's feelings are valid, they don't have permission to be disrespectful while expressing their
feelings.

So, when one of my kids is having a Code 12
while under my explicit care, I engage the child,
not their unacceptable behavior. The child not getting what they want at that moment is the root of
most Code 12s. They cannot accept their reality at
the moment. They also can't think of alternatives.
So, as parents and guardians, we have to help
them navigate the process.

Code 12s can manifest in different ways at various ages. With the two-year-old in my story, it
was a change in his breakfast routine. That slight
change turned on torrential tears! For a six-year-
old in the middle of Walmart, being told they can't
have a toy can cause them to throw a tantrum. For
a thirteen-year-old being denied the privilege of
sleeping over at a friend's house, they can launch a
verbal assault that ends with "I wish you weren't
my parents!" and a bedroom door slamming.

No matter what their age or situation, just remember that at the root of a Code 12, the child

feels as though they have no options for getting what they want, so they are acting out. For a peaceful resolution, don't engage the behavior; engage the child. Then, give them other options and allow them to make their own choice from the possibilities you present.

That's what I did with the two-year-old in my story. Instead of asking him to stop crying or matching his expressions of frustration with my own, I ignored his behavior and addressed the real issue. I talked to him in a calm voice, which was opposite to his own. I never had to ask him to stop crying because he became engaged in our conversation. During the exchange, he stopped fixating on what he didn't have, the root cause of his frustration. Asking him what he wanted me to buy from the supermarket later gave him a chance to cast a vote for breakfast options. It was a stark contrast from being forced to accept a non-negotiable choice. By asking him questions, I found out what else he was interested in eating for breakfast. Once I knew what else he liked, I gave him the chance to choose it for himself. Once he knew he was about to eat something he wanted, he didn't mind eating the fruit when asked.

Yes, I straight up Jedi Mind Tricked him into

doing what his parents wanted him to do, because I couldn't let him play his parents like that. There is no shame in my game. I will steal points from kids!

I know this may be a lot to absorb. You may find it challenging to remember these steps during a heated moment. The good news? You only need to remember three points:

1. Don't engage the behavior; engage the child. Help them stop fixating on what they don't have or can't do.
2. Find out what other preapproved options they might prefer.
3. Allow them to make their own choice.

Don't feel bad if, during your next Code 12, you only remember one out of the three steps. Stay calm and try it again next time. I promise you this: the first time you execute these steps successfully, the unacceptable behavior will magically stop. You'll think you are Merlin the Magician! And when that happens, you can reward yourself with an enchanted elixir: a shot of Irish cream and cognac. If it was an unusually long and loud Code 12, reach for a chardonnay so you can get a really good buzz!

Chapter 3

Code 13: A Full-On Tantrum (a.k.a. Code 12 + 1)

You now know a tantrum—a.k.a. a Code 12—is when a kid starts with the weeping, wailing, and gnashing of teeth. Well, a "full-on tantrum" is a Code 12 + 1 . . . literally! It is a tantrum that has gone to the next level. Code 13s typically don't just materialize out of thin air. Nine times out of ten, they start out as a Code 12, and then escalate to out-of-control proportions.

A Code 13 is usually a full-body experience beyond just crying or screaming. The kid drops to the floor like an anvil and feels just as heavy if you try to lift them. They might roll around or spin on their head like they're a breakdancer. They throw things. They'll kick anybody unlucky enough to be in the way.

There is just no consoling the child in a full-blown Code 13. You can't stop it. You can't break it. You can't make friends with it. It takes over and has the nerve to go on and on. It shuts down everybody's situation, and it's a wrap on your sanity.

You know exactly what I'm talking about. Just thinking of it makes you want to reach for your shot of bourbon right now . . . maybe even two! But, not yet. You must first learn to shut down a Code 13 successfully. So, how do I make a Code 13 stop?

I walk away from it.

I know you're probably thinking, *Seriously? Just walk away? Ha! I've tried that before, and it didn't stop them from continuing to carry on.* Want to know why they kept going? Because you went back to them five seconds later, got in their face again, and yelled at them to stop, didn't you? You engaged the behavior and not the child, so the Code 13 continued.

I will admit, I oversimplified. There is a particular way in which I walk away from a Code 13. But, before I share this story, here is something you need to know: I have an arsenal of tools and go-to tricks I use with my families. One activity I often introduce is making natural, fruit-based popsicles. The kids love the fun of preparing them, and the ingredients usually go over well with health-conscious parents. To be honest, I do it because not having kids hyped up on high-fructose corn syrup makes my job easier!

One summer afternoon, I was on duty caring for a five-year-old girl and her brother. This day, we had just enough popsicles for her, her brother, Mom, and me; there were none left in the freezer. So, we took our popsicles out to the backyard. The five-year-old and her brother ran around, playing and giggling, while holding their popsicles in their hands. Everything was fine until she bumped into the outdoor couch, causing her to loosen her grip on the popsicle. It went tumbling to the ground on a patch of dirt and mulch-filled landscaping. Not only that, when it fell, it shattered into a bunch of small chunks. They were impossible to pick up and salvage.

Cue the high-pitched, horror movie, shrieking

violins! Popsicle down! It was a wrap! When the popsicle met its end, that is where she began! I saw terror wash over the little girl's face, and I braced for impact.

Remember how I said earlier that nine times out of ten, a Code 13 usually starts off as a Code 12? Well, this was that tenth time! It did not pass Go. It did not collect $200. And, it did not make a pit stop at Code 12. My girl went from 0 to Code 13 in an instant!

At once she let out a howl that could have scared a coyote! She dropped to the ground (maybe it was a futile attempt at salvaging the itsy-bitsy pieces) and launched a certified fit. First, her popsicle was history. Second, she knew there were none left. And finally, since she was a part of the process of making them, she knew they take a while to make. She had no possibility of enjoying a popsicle at that moment. Needless to say, she was inconsolable. Mom tried bargaining and reasoning with her to no avail. After a few more minutes, Mom grew frustrated. She threatened, "Well, if you continue acting this way, then we won't make popsicles again."

At that point, my five-year-old wasn't trying to hear that. Mom's empty threat made her even more upset. Mom looked at me with a look on her face that said, "Do you have any bright ideas?" The Code 13 showed no signs of letting up soon.

I walked over to where the little girl was and called her name in a calm voice. "You're having a Code 13," I said, "and I need you to get up off the ground. It will be okay. I'm going into the kitchen to slice up oranges to make more popsicles for next time. If you want to join me, you can come. But, you can't come while you're crying. You've got to be a big girl." Then I walked off toward the kitchen and left her there.

As soon as I turned my back, I heard the impact of my words. The crying and howling immediately stopped. She heard "more popsicles," and to her, it was like I was giving her a replacement for her destroyed popsicle, even if it wasn't instant gratification. That was enough for her to pull herself together.

As I stood in the kitchen prepping the oranges for the blender, I heard a sweet, calm voice behind me say, "MeMi, can I help you pour it into the popsicle containers?"

I had to contain my chuckle in front of her. "Absolutely!" I responded. "And when you're done, you can also put in the stick." After we put them in full molds in the freezer, I asked her,

"Are you ready to go back outside and play?"

"Yes," she answered joyfully, and off she went. It was as if the Code 13 never happened.

It never ceases to amaze me how kids can go from a Code 12 or Code 13 back to normal in a snap. Mom and I were thrilled to see her happy-go-lucky attitude again. We survived the moment!

That's what you want to do: survive! Both you and the kids need to get past those moments of unbearable tension. Your desire is for your kids to just stop their lashing out. Keep in mind that they can't "just stop." No ma'am, Pam! They have to take the long way around to "just stop." They have to get on a bus, transfer to a train, then call an Uber from the station before they can arrive home at "just stop!"

Remember, when a child fixates on what they can't have, they will act out and perform a Code 13 for you. Their current reality is bleak, so they feel frustrated. They can't think up a workable alternative. So, we as adults must help them along and speed up the process.

Let me break down my Code 13 survival tricks

for you. It is a modified version of how I deal with a Code 12, so it should be a little familiar.

1. Don't engage the unacceptable behavior; engage the child.
2. Communicate your expectations and give them a choice.
3. Walk away and let them make their decision.

First, don't engage the unacceptable behavior. I called my five-year-old's name in a calm voice and laid out my expectation for her. She had to get up off the ground. Second, I gave her a choice. I opened the door for her to help me make more popsicles with a specific condition. Finally, I walked away. I gave her the space to decide on her own. She could have followed me into the kitchen, or she could have continued crying and carrying on.

As with a Code 12, a parent's typical knee-jerk reaction to a Code 13 usually fuels the fire. Remember Mom yelling, bargaining, and threatening to take away privileges? It didn't work. It *never* works. No matter how tempted I am, I've trained myself to not argue with children, nor do I acknowledge their tantrums. Don't feed into the negative energy, because they'll keep the tantrum going when you do. Kids throwing a Code 13 love and feed off of an audience. So, don't give them one.

The hardest part for parents in implementing my Code 13 survival tactics is turning a deaf ear to the crying and unnecessary antics. Remember that kids often use crying as a manipulation tactic. It is one of the first things they learn as babies. Think if it: when they cried, you magically appeared and attended to them. As kids get older, they continue turning on the waterworks because they know you'll respond to it.

Become vigilant.

Unless they are crying because they actually hurt themselves, you must ignore it. Train yourself to not respond when they are crying because they're not getting their way. You don't want to respond to or engage this behavior. The minute you do, you've lost control.

When you practice walking away from a Code 12, resist the urge to go back and face them if they are still crying a few minutes after you have initially walked away. Also, if the Code 13 is because you have said no to their request, you must make sure you don't change your "no" into a "yes" ten minutes later just because you want them to stop. It will end the Code 13 in the short term, yes, but now they'll be thinking, *If I misbehave and carry on long enough, Mom/Dad/Nana/Papa will change their mind, and I'll get what I originally wanted!* Then, the next time you walk into a Code 13, they will already have a point up on the board, and you will have lost before you even begin. You'll be playing their game, and you will give into them again.

When you walk away from a Code 13 in progress like you mean it, it messes with a kid's mind! Once they realize there is no audience to perform for, they usually calm down and change direction. Once they receive a viable substitute for what they are missing or can't have, the Code 13 stops on its own.

That is the real key to successfully ending a Code 13. The child must feel as if they are getting a good substitute for what they originally wanted. Once satisfied, the Code 13 shuts off like a light switch. Kids then proceed as if nothing ever happened. They'll break out into a song! They'll go back to playing peacefully, or they'll color in an activity book. Sometimes they shake it off, find me, and ask, "MeMi, can I have some water?" That's when I know it's over and I survived another Code 13!

Don't feel bad if you try this technique and don't get the results you're looking for the first time. I know you're tired, you're working, and you've already had a long day. Just be persistent and try your best to maintain your sanity. Then you'll be able to think of a good substitution for what they want that you approve of. When that moment happens, you'll know, and *then* you'll be ready for your shot of bourbon—maybe two!

Chapter 4

Code 14: Frozen (a.k.a. Let It Go)

I don't know about you, but after dealing with Code 12 and Code 13, I'm exhausted, and I need a change of pace! Good thing Code 14 is next . . . but I'm not sure you will care for this one.

Code 14 isn't a discipline technique for kids. While they commit plenty of infractions throughout the day worthy of me writing tickets for, kids are not the only offenders in the house. Sometimes I have to write up tickets for parents' unacceptable behaviors, and Code 14 is one of the most significant parental offenses. Code 14 is introducing your child to a sport or activity and it doesn't work out.

Now, before you close the book and stop reading, hear me out! I'm not trying to low-key call you a bad parent. Remember, I hold anyone in high regard who willingly commits to the sacrifices parenting requires. But, just because we are adults doesn't mean we always get everything right.

It is great to have goals and dreams for your kids. However, adults need to remember that kids have their own goals and dreams. They know their own minds. They will tell you their preferences if you ask them. Don't forget, I am a stranger who gets to go into people's homes, so I see a lot! I've seen unnecessary conflicts arise between parents and children just because Mom or Dad is forcing Johnny or Sally to take part in an extracurricular activity that doesn't suit them.

Don't get me wrong—there are a few non-negotiables for kids. They must go to school. They must learn to read, write, and do arithmetic. They must be respectful to everyone. As parents or guardians, our job is to ensure the children in our care adequately advance in these areas. Yet, when it comes to extracurricular activities, such as being involved in music, other arts, or sports, I believe parents and guardians should get their kid's input, or at least interpret the subtle signs your child is giving you.

For example, if your son refuses to come out of the dugout when it's time for the team to line up for batting practice, that's a sign. If your daughter's pirouette looks more like a lazy half-twirl after five years of ballet, that's a sign. When your twin boys are on the side of the soccer field making up their own game instead of playing with the team on the field, that's a sign. Your daughter still can't do a cartwheel after six years of gymnastics? That is most definitely a sign to let it go!

Stop forcing your uninterested child to take these classes. Obviously, you are not getting a return on your investment! I call Code 14 "Frozen" because sometimes parents, just like the song from the famous Disney movie, just have to "let it go!"

I know a few of my examples might sound hilarious to you, but keep in mind, they are based on real events! Although I might anonymize names or fictionalize a few details to protect the innocent and my job, that gymnastics situation is a #truestory!

The star of this story is a lovely young sixteen-year-old we'll call Elsa. Her mom took gymnastics as a child, so she had golden Olympic rings in her eyes when she signed Elsa up for her first gymnastics class when she was just five years old.

When I began my tenure with Elsa's family, she had already been in gymnastics for a few years. Mom talked proudly about her daughter's progress, but then I accompanied Elsa to one of her meets. Elsa legitimately struggled through each of her routines, bless her heart. Her tumbling looked painful, her balance beam was worse, and she couldn't do a cartwheel with straight knees to save her life. Gymnastics was apparently not her calling, and the Olympics was never going to happen. Yet, Mom kept signing her up year . . . after year . . . after year!

About two years in, I worked up the courage to ask Elsa directly if she liked gymnastics. She told me how she enjoyed her friends, the sleepovers, and the pizza parties her team had, but Elsa never said she liked the sport itself. Season after season, Elsa's lack of improvement was apparent to everyone except Mom. It is possible, of course, that Elsa was pretending to not excel in hopes Mom would catch the hint and not sign her up again. Either way, gymnastics wasn't her passion.

But guess what was? Hip-hop dancing. That, Elsa absolutely loved! Her dance team had the chance to perform at an NBA game last year, and I caught her show. I thought she was the best one on the floor (and not just because she's my baby!). Elsa had fantastic energy, great facial expressions, and her moves were on point. I was so proud of her! I was watching an entirely different Elsa. This Elsa was alive and loving every minute of what she was doing. I later learned that for her to get her dance classes, Mom insisted that she still take gymnastics, too. Mom needed a ticket written up for violating Code 14! Her sentence? Listen to the song "Let It Go" five times in a row!

I had another family who ignored the smoke signals their son was sending them. Every Saturday, we loaded up into the SUV and headed off to the soccer field. And every Saturday, the little boy pulled his hat over his eyes and moaned in the back seat. When it was time to be on the field, he wouldn't go. He stayed off to the side and played with another teammate who equally disliked the game.

Dad signed him up again for a second year, and then again for a third! He thought the discipline could help build his character. The third season was torturous for the little boy because it was indoor soccer. There was no such thing as a rained-out game! And, he still wouldn't go on the field during practice. Instead, he ran around the gym, making up his own games with whoever would play. They played catch, tag, or whatever they wanted, and were having the time of their lives!

Meanwhile, the coach was fuming. It was tough to keep the rest of the team focused because the little boy's fun was contagious. The rest of the team wanted to play with him! Soccer was not engaging for him, and his sideline antics disrupted everyone else's productivity. The signs couldn't be more obvious that this little boy was not interested in soccer. Dad needed three tickets written up for violating Code 14, one for each year wasted on this futile effort.

If you're tempted to stop reading, may I remind you, I haven't gotten to your drink yet for this chapter! It's coming soon, I promise!

Look, I'm not trying to tell you how to raise your children. I'm just sharing with you my observations. I think it's great to encourage participation, but I think you should also heed the signs and allow your kids some choice in what they take part in.

I know the tendency is to start kids young in

various activities, such as ballet or soccer, at three and four years old. But, even at that age, they can tell you if they like it or not if you ask them. Remember our two-year-old boy and the cereal? When asked, even he could say what else he wanted for breakfast.

I can understand if you've already paid for an activity for the year and you want to help your children understand the value of seeing a commitment through to the end. However, if you know they are not enjoying the activity or you are not seeing any progress in their skill level, then it may be time to "let it go." Try another activity next season; they might enjoy it more. Don't continue forcing them because it's something you did as a child, or you are secretly (or blatantly) hoping it will turn into a professional career for them. It rarely ends well for your relationship with your child.

I know this chapter is a tough pill to swallow. So, I give you permission to chase it down with a martini. Make it dirty or wet if you're feeling the irony of the situation, or have it perfect or dry if you're still licking your wounds and coming to terms with letting go.

Chapter 5

Code 15: Sippy Cup Is Community Property

Alrighty then, enough about you! We are now returning to the regular format of this book: nipping kids' offenses in the bud! Code 15 is how everything from car seats, toys, snacks, and even sippy cups can be shared among siblings.

Code 15 is all about sharing, and we know how much kids love to share—NOT! Toddlers' favorite word is "no." Their second favorite word is "mine." Families who have multiple children, especially if they are close in age, will easily relate to Code 15! If, on the other hand, you are a parent of an only child, pay close attention, too, because when they have friends or cousins their age over and get into brawls, you'll want to use these techniques to break up any issues that arise from the lack of sharing.

So, what exactly does "sippy cup is community property" mean?

Let's say I'm out with a family at a Disney show, and Mom and Day purchased one big drink (because you know it's expensive!) for the kids to share. Everyone is not getting their own drink because it's both cost prohibitive and too much for one child to drink alone. So, we will pass the big drink down and share. Sippy cup is community property!

If a sibling forgets their sippy cup at the park by accident, then someone else has to share theirs. Sippy cup is community property.

If we're in the car and one child tosses their sippy cup out the window (#truestory) and someone else gets thirsty, there's no luxury of "mine." Everyone has to drink out of what is available. Sippy cup is community property.

Now, I'm not in favor of kids sharing their

germs. Having multiple small kids sick with a cold at the same time is totally not fun. So, I have evolved my tactics by purchasing the same sippy cups for all the small ones in a family, then I write the first initial of their name on the bottom. It helps them with letter recognition, and they can help themselves to their own cup. But, in case of emergency, the sippy cup is community property, and they all look the same!

This concept applies not only to sippy cups. Snacks are community property. Your diaper bag is community property. Your toys. EVERYTHING is community property!

I don't give in to children when they whine about how their brother or sister stole their toy or ate their snack. If someone left something at home or on the playground, I ask the other sibling to share. I consciously work on teaching kids in my care that "sharing is caring." My goal is to help them learn that anything they have, they can share it with someone else, and everyone can be happy and get along. Once they understand that I expect them to share amongst themselves, it drastically cuts down on the sibling fights (Code 17), meltdowns (Codes 12 and 13), and all-out catastrophes (Code 57/11).

Being a nanny is not just a job for me to collect a paycheck. I am genuinely concerned about shaping young children into amazing adults. I want to help them form language and coping skills early. My philosophy is that giving is part of the heart. If a child continually hears, "This is mine, go get your own stuff," or, "No, I don't want to share with you," what is that going to do for their self-esteem?

Beyond that, they will probably pass on the same sentiments to their peers when they are at school, church, or in other community settings as they continue to grow up. They will mature into adults who are only concerned about themselves. It might seem minor to help children share their toys or snacks, but I see it as an essential early building block in learning how to care for and have compassion and empathy for others. If we want our kids to grow up to be concerned citizens who are engaged in positively shaping our society, the lessons start young, and they start at home.

But enough of me on my soapbox! I know you want to hear a juicy Code 15 story, right? Okay, here's one for you, and it involves an only child.

Once, I was caring for a seven-year-old boy who liked having play dates with his friends. Yet, whenever his friends came over, he turned bossy, telling them *which* toy he wanted them to play with and *how* they should play. Plus, he always changed the rules in the middle of games to suit himself. It was overkill! The friends never appreciated it, so playing often dissolved into fighting.

My kid knew my Codes. Whenever I saw a play date heading south, I could quickly put the kibosh on the situation. I only needed to walk up to them and say to my seven-year-old, "Are we having a Code 15? Does our friend need to get in the car so I can take him home?"

The threat of the playdate being over was usually an excellent way to help him regain perspective. His eyes would go wide and he'd stammer, "No, MeMi! We're playing real good. I really want him to stay."

I would continually remind him, "Your friend is a guest in your home. Show him your toys and ask him, 'What do you want to play with?' Don't force him to do only what you want. Because *why*?"

I'd wait, then usually get the response in a mumbled voice, "Because sharing is caring."

As I'm sure you know, getting kids used to sharing does not happen overnight. You as the adult must continually reinforce the principle. I get tickled whenever my kids get into an argument with their sibling. They throw everything I've taught them back at each other. I definitely hear them checking each other by saying, "You're not sharing! Sharing is caring!" Other times I'll hear, "You're not being kind! Those unkind words will not yield kind actions!" My kids make me giggle because it's precious, but it also lets me know they are listening and are trying to resolve their problems among themselves.

I don't have a cute three-step process for you to follow on a Code 15. When I see an infraction in progress where two siblings or friends are fussing at each other because someone is refusing to share, I merely tell them, "Code 15. Community property. Share!" Something else I like to say is, "Bro-bro, talk it out, work it out." I then walk away to let them work it out, but I stay close enough to hear what's happening in case I need to mediate. Once kids know they're expected to resolve their conflicts themselves, they usually do. But, I'm getting a little ahead of myself. You'll learn more about that phrase and technique in Chapter 7, where I discuss Code 17.

The moment you hear your kids talking through their differences and coming up with a solution to sharing on their own, you will know you have conquered Code 15. It is a sweet victory, so I say you have permission to enjoy a nice, fruity daiquiri at the end of your day.

Chapter 6

Code 16: Get In Where You Fit In

R arely are things "assigned" in a child's life, be it seating or particular cups to use. This is where the lesson from Code 16 comes in: get in where you fit in! A Code 16 happens when kids fight over things that are not assigned. In keeping with the theme of this chapter, let's jump right into a story that illustrates a Code 16 perfectly!

First, here's the setup: we have a seven-year-old boy, a five-year-old girl, and a four-year-old boy. The family had a full-sized SUV with a third row. The parents installed identical car seats for the youngest two: one in the middle row and one in the back row next to the driver's-side window. For whatever reason, sitting in this back-row car seat was to the kids like Zeus sitting on his throne atop Mt. Olympus. You would think sitting in this particular seat gave them superhero powers or something!

Can you start to picture in your mind where we're headed? When I began my tenure with this family, the following was typical every time we got ready to go out. It could play out over an exhausting fifteen or twenty minutes, and we were always late to wherever we were going. The victor varied daily, but the scene might happen like this . . .

(Cue the action!)

I walked down the stairs toward the door with my backpack (to prevent a Code 11), prepared for our destination. The kids were already in the foyer in various stages of putting on shoes and jackets. Dad appeared from the formal living room, grabbed the car keys by the door, and said, "Okay, kids, let's go!"

Those words were as if the "Round One" bell

just rang! In unison, six pairs of eyes popped wide open as they momentarily froze in their tracks. The same thought hit each child at once: *I must be THE ONE to reach the back row first!*

(Cue the slow-motion bionic running-sound effect!)

Dad opened the front door and released the thoroughbreds! The seven-year-old shot out the door like a cannon. He didn't need to fight for the other seat in the back row, so I always wondered why he ran. Maybe he just liked the thrill of the chase, I don't know. A halfway put-on jacket flew like a flag on one pumping arm as he sped down the path.

His five-year-old sister was right on his heels. His sleeve flapped in her face. Annoyed, she swatted it out of her way.

An untied shoelace tripped the four-year-old bringing up the rear. He fell further behind. But then he saw his sister ready to claim THE ONE car seat in the back row, so he persevered. He hopped out of the problem shoe, leaving it on the pathway.

Meanwhile, the five-year-old got slick and grabbed hold of her older brother's flapping jacket. She yanked him back and used the momentum to propel herself into the lead. In her mind, her older brother could not stand in the way of her triumph over her younger brother. The middle child must come first in something, right? She reached the car-door handle first.

With an assumed victory in her sights, she didn't see her older brother recover from his stumble and reach for her leg as she was trying to scramble into the car. The two tussled in between the seats. The determined four-year-old reached the SUV. He took advantage of the scuffle and tried to climb on top of his distracted siblings to get to the back seat first.

Now the five-year-old got really mad at her older brother for slowing her down, and the older brother didn't appreciate the four-year-old's knee in his side. It was an all-out war between the three. Their yelps filled the air in the front yard. The parked SUV rocked back and forth under the weight of their WWE-worthy brawl. I tried jumping in to peel the kids off of each other so they wouldn't hurt themselves. But, whenever I grabbed one, the other two made a beeline for the throne.

By this point, Mom or Dad thundered out the front door and yelled, "What's going on out here? What are you all doing?" As if this didn't happen every day! For just a moment, parental presence paused the action. Then someone wiggled into the back seat. The action resumed. Parental presence no longer a concern, the other two pounced to eject the victor, who was already working on strapping themselves into the throne.

I bet you're ready for that drink now, aren't you? Not yet; we still have a way to go! Because even though someone had become THE ONE, the battle wasn't necessarily over. There were plenty of arguments, tears, complaining, threats of time-out, and lots of coaxing to get "the loser" into the empty middle-row car seat. It was always an exhausting ordeal before we could even put the car into gear!

Remember, these battle royales occurred whenever the whole family traveled anywhere. There were several ways that Mom, Dad, and I tried to handle these daily scrimmages early on. I used to sneak the kids out of the house one at a time. I put the first child into the back seat because, logistically, it was easier. That wasn't an acceptable solution, though, because the other child would have a Code 12 in response.

We tried assigned seating. That didn't work, either. The other kid whined all the way to the destination and back while THE ONE unleashed a torrent of teasing on "the loser." We tried rotating seat assignments, but it became too complicated to remember who sat where during the last ride. Asking the kids wasn't helpful. I mean, do you really think they told the truth?

One day I was taking the kids out for ice cream by myself. The bickering was way too much for me. I was over it. I interrupted the arguing with an authoritative, "Just find an empty seat and buckle up! Get in where you fit in!" It is possible they were tired of the fighting, too, because to my surprise, they complied. They grumbled, but they settled down and found a seat.

A lightbulb turned on in my head, and Code 16 was born. Whatever was available, they had to "get in where they fit in" and not fight. I quickly realized that my new Code was very similar to the sharing concept I teach in Code 15. And like Code 15, I discovered that "get in where you fit in" applied to more than just car seats.

If a scooter isn't occupied, you may play with it. Get in where you fit in. If identical snacks are on the table, pick one up and eat it. Get in where you fit in. When I take the kids to the park, nobody likes to wait to slide or swing. But I always whisper in my kids' ears, "You see that line? Wait your turn like everyone else. Get in where you fit in!" It even applies to games! When playing a game of freeze tag, for example, no one ever likes to be "out." But, kids must learn to abide by the rules. They can't jump back into the game whenever they want to; they must wait on the sidelines for the game to finish. When another round starts up, they can join in again.

Kids resist this idea at first. They love having their own way. They always want something to be "mine." Frankly, it is that "mine" mindset that makes me drink around seven p.m. every day if I'm off the clock! But, once kids get used to my expectations around Code 16, "get in where you fit in" nips that "mine" disease in the bud. Code 16 helps kids learn patience and timing while re-inforcing sharing. Small children five and under haven't yet developed a sense of time, as they haven't fully grasped numbers yet. However, they can learn that they must exercise patience and wait their turn. It's not what they want to do, but eventually they get it.

Code 16 also helps kids learn to consider others when they are in different environments outside of their home. When they are at school or on the playground, they are not just interacting with their family who might give in to their demands. Children must develop coping skills to deal with situations that are not going their way. The concept behind "get in where you fit in" does the trick.

Similar to Code 15, there is no quick "three-step system." The next time a Code 16 occurs, use that moment to explain what "get in where you fit in" means. Express what behavior you are expecting of them when you use that phrase. Then, reinforce it. Getting kids to comply with Code 16 on their own will take patience on your part as a parent, grandparent, or guardian. But once kids understand what you mean when you tell them, "Get in where you fit in," they will begin exhibiting more patient and compassionate behavior. If they comply begrudgingly or with complaints, don't worry about it. As long as sibling wars get nipped in the bud when you utter this magical phrase, you are welcome to enjoy a margarita at the end of your day!

Chapter 7

Code 17: Someone's Not Playing Well with Others

ode 17 is when one or more children are not playing well with others. Do you have multiple children close in age in your household? You'll probably be shouting out "Code 17!" at the kids all day once you get the hang of it! Although it takes kids a while to get used to Codes 15 and 16, they latch on to Code 17 right away. Why? Because of all the Codes, Code 17 affects their daily existence the most!

It always cracks me up to see a three-year-old

run behind their older sibling yelling, "Code 17!", or when they come snitching, saying, "MiMe, MiMe! She took my toy. She's not playing well with others!" I usually need to straighten my face before I step in as sheriff to help mediate.

But, I'm getting a little ahead of myself.

Code 17 encompasses those sibling fights that always erupt when one gets into "mine" mode and doesn't want to share. It can also apply when one child is being bossy and not giving others a chance. Boy, do I have an epic, Tarantino-worthy tale to tell you! I'm sure you've seen a version of the following story play out in your own household.

One afternoon, two brothers close in age were playing independently. Let's call them Batman and Robin. Robin was in the family room building a tower with Legos®. Batman came into the room where Robin was playing. He was playing with Legos, too, in a different room, and he wanted to build something with one specific block that Robin had already worked into his tower. Rather than find something else to play with, Batman decided he couldn't live without that one particular piece. So, he tried taking it from Robin.

Robin was having none of it! The two started

brawling. I'm talking arms and legs tangled up, rolling around on the floor–type of fighting. If they were in a wrestling ring, one of them would have gotten up on the ropes and performed a flying body slam on the other!

The tussling destroyed Robin's tower. Robin zoomed past Code 12 and immediately launched into a Code 13. At that point, I could have stepped in, but a beautiful thing happened. See, these kids knew my Codes. Batman knew he was wrong for making his brother cry. So, he tried making peace. As I hinted back in Code 15, my solution for a Code 17 is my phrase "Bro-bro, talk it out, work it out." And that is exactly what they did.

I was proud to see them calmly talk to each other. They agreed Robin should keep the coveted Lego piece, because he had it first. Batman left to go back to playing in his room. All was well . . . but only for a few minutes! Even though Batman initially walked away, he still wanted that one particular piece pretty badly.

Soon enough, Batman meandered back into the family room innocently. And, when he thought Robin wasn't looking, he stole the coveted piece from the rubble of the destroyed tower. But Robin couldn't be punked! He realized what Batman did. His anger reignited. The family room became a boxing ring again, and it was Round Two!

Here is where the plot thickens. Batman assessed his situation. He still didn't have what he wanted, and he couldn't escape his brother's blows. If he wanted to win the war, he needed reinforcement. So, Batman left the room to go recruit Mom and Dad. Within a few minutes, Mom and Dad charged into the family room, upset with Robin. They yelled at Robin for fighting with Batman over a Lego piece. Apparently, Batman left out the part of the story where Robin had it first. He also didn't admit he was trying to steal the piece, which is what caused the fighting to begin with.

Poor Robin! He tried to defend himself as best he could by telling his parents what really happened, but Mom and Dad were wearing invisible Team Batman shirts, because they said, "It's okay, Robin. Batman is playing with the piece now. You can wait your turn."

The injustice of that statement made Robin launch into a Code 12. He cried and whined that he was the one who had the piece first. Mom and Dad's response? They argued back and forth with Robin, still advocating for Batman. Meanwhile,

Batman had slunk into the background and was playing with the stolen Lego piece. In a fit of frustration, Robin snatched the offending Lego piece back from Batman's possession.

Batman's response? He started Code 12ing too! Since no one asked for my input, I had to watch the drama unfold until, finally, both boys stormed out to their respective rooms, and no one was playing with Legos. I told you this one was epic!

Parents and guardians can throw serious fuel on the fire of a Code 17 by taking sides without hearing all the facts. Here, my parents were going hard for Batman's story, defending him against Robin as if they were eyewitnesses! I mean, Mom and Dad were ready to march and protest for "the cause" like they were activists! "Give. It. Back!" they kept yelling at Robin, speaking about the Lego piece in question. "We're not leaving until you give it back!" they threatened. The danger in taking sides is, the one who is telling the truth might feel as though truth means nothing because the liar will be defended.

So, how would I resolve this Code 17? As I mentioned, there was an early moment where the kids had enacted my solution to a Code 17. They used my saying, "Bro-bro, talk it out, work it out." It means exactly what it says. Siblings must talk to each other and come to a resolution on their own. This ensures they both will agree on the solution. Batman and Robin went through this process and came to an agreement. The problem is, one person chose not to abide by the truce. So, they needed the opportunity to do it again. They could have repeatedly agreed on the Lego piece until the agreement stuck.

But, Batman took his slyness up a few notches by involving their parents. If I were Mom or Dad, invited into an incident I had not witnessed from the beginning, I would not take sides. I would have listened to Batman's version of the story, but upon entering the family room, I'd ask Robin for his side. Ultimately, my tactic is mediation. My strategy is to guide kids into working out their differences with each other. This gives them the opportunity to practice real-world coping skills they'll need later in life.

As adults, we don't always need to intervene in sibling conflicts and dictate what happens. When you examine it, playing with toys should be fun, but during moments of tension, feelings can be hurt and resentments can build. Similar to helping children realize that sharing is caring from Codes 15 and 16, we as adults can help children exercise independence and allow them to develop negotiating and conflict-resolution skills during a Code 17. Besides, when children resolve their own issues, they are empowered. They love knowing they can do something meaningful on their own.

Not playing well with each other is a recurring thing. It's something that goes away and comes back. This is not a one-and-done type of deal. It will take a long time for the kids to get used to playing well with each other. Even if they come up with a decision together, they might change their minds, as Batman did earlier. But, when you have moments when they do work out their problems on their own, you can count it as a victory. So, for this code, you probably should keep a White Russian on hand at all times so you can sip on it throughout the day!

Chapter 8

Code 18: Laundry Drama

Code 18 is when the never-ending laundry task unexpectedly becomes dramatic. This is the shortest chapter in the book because it's an "open and shut" case. Similar to Code 14 (Let It Go), Code 18 is more about adults' ticket-worthy behavior than the children's. I mean, it's called laundry drama. Your kids can't do laundry yet!

Laundry drama happens when adults are ill-prepared on the clean-clothes-and-linen front. And, when the adults fall behind on the job, the kids usually suffer the consequence. In my world, laundry drama often results in naked kids!

During my first year of being a nanny, I had a funny experience. I was a few days into a new assignment caring for a ten-month-old baby boy. My plan was to take him out to the park and tire him out. He already had his sippy cup in his hand. The diaper bag was by the door, so I picked it up and we left. (The diaper bag was Kate Spade, by the way. This detail will become important later.) Not long into our time at the park, the little boy paused for a moment with a focused look on his face. Then he smiled and resumed playing. It didn't take long for me to smell what he had done.

I took him back to the car. I had wipes on me in my personal bag, so I got him squeaky clean. Next, I unzipped the diaper bag with my free hand and reached in . . . but I couldn't feel any diapers! I didn't feel a change of clothes, either. I looked inside the bag in disbelief. The only thing in the bag was a rattle and Mom's makeup bag! I didn't know what to do, so I put the naked baby into his car seat and drove back home. I hoped that because he had just pooped, he'd at least make it back to the house without urinating. But, halfway through the five-minute ride, I heard soft and steady whizzing on the car's upholstery!

When I stepped back into the house with a naked baby in my arms, Mom looked horrified. "What happened?" she asked.

After I explained my dilemma, emphasizing that there were no supplies in the diaper bag, she got wide-eyed and she giggled. "You know what?" she laughed. "We went to a concert last night, and we used that bag to sneak in a bottle of wine and glasses! We forgot to put the baby's stuff back in the bag. I am so sorry!"

Because the Kate Spade diaper bag looked very much like a woman's purse, they got away with it. I was just relieved that it wasn't an oversight on my part and I wasn't in jeopardy of losing my new gig. But, that situation taught me an early lesson. It is why I am always prepared with my own supplies for the kids in my care.

My current employer always teases me by saying, "Why do you carry so many bags with you?"

I already told you about my backpack full of goodies that I carry everywhere to keep the kids occupied, hydrated, and fed. Well, that's not the only bag I carry with me. I carry a second bag with extra changes of clothes, underwear, and diapers if I am caring for children five and under. I also keep a few first-aid supplies in it, as well.

In response to my current employer's question, I turned to her and said, "In the four years I've worked for you, when have you ever needed anything when I was with you?"

Her silence was her answer. Listen, I like to be prepared (remember Code 11?). I prepare for worst-case scenarios because, with kids around, the worst-case scenario usually happens at least once a day. Whenever I am out with any of my families, we never run to the drugstore for a bottle of water, antibiotic ointment, band-aids—nothing! My mentality is anything (especially laundry drama) can happen at any time and in the most inconvenient places. It's all traced back to the empty Kate Spade diaper bag!

So, I already gave you one example of laundry drama. What are other examples? Let's say you are out with a child that isn't 100 percent potty-trained yet. If she didn't quite make it to the bathroom on time and you don't have a change of clothes handy, that is laundry drama! When a four-year-old falls asleep in the car and accidentally wets him or herself because traffic is crazier than expected (which is every day in the Metro Atlanta area), that is laundry drama, too.

Laundry drama can happen inside the home,

as well. Did your baby ever make a mess while you were preparing them for bed? Have you ever tried to change the sheets, only to discover all the linens are dirty? That's laundry drama! Or, maybe you started laundry late, so the sheets aren't dry by bedtime. If you've ever laid your kid to sleep on top of a blanket, you know you've experienced laundry drama!

And don't think laundry drama is limited to babies and toddlers. Just forget to wash your seven-year-old boy's favorite superhero pajamas and ask him to wear something else to bed. You'll have a Code 12 on your hands faster than Spider-Man can sling a web!

The only way around laundry drama is to just do it, or make sure it's always done. Alternatively, you can keep duplicates of your kids' favorite outfits so they don't launch into a Code 12 when it's dirty!

I know, I know, nobody likes to do laundry. Unfortunately, it's a constant, dreaded duty, especially from birth to twenty-four months. Parents of newborns go through onesies like Jennifer Lopez changing outfits in a Vegas show: at least five times per hour! And older kids have a tendency to love one particular outfit, PJ set, or costume, and will wear it to death if you let them, no matter how dirty, grungy, linty, balled up, or shrunken it gets!

My prescription for minimizing laundry drama is to always pack extra clothes for kids five and under whenever you leave the house. Be sure to stay on top of your laundry schedule to make sure all the older kids' favorite clothes and linens are clean. Once the kids are tucked in, sip on a glass of calming white wine as you listen to the soft whirl of the washer and hum of the dryer!

Chapter 9

Code 19: The Witching Hour

C ode 19 is that rough patch between dinner and bedtime that I call "the Witching Hour." The child can't be consoled because they are tired from their day, but still have a couple of hours to stay awake before bedtime. Just when you are looking forward to the end of a day full of Code 13s, Code 17s, and a mini-meltdown over laundry drama, you'll quickly realize that it's not over yet. If it's after five p.m., you've just entered the Witching Hour!

I call the time between five p.m. and bedtime the Witching Hour because just about anything that can happen, will happen! This is a peculiar time of day where kids—particularly toddlers and younger—are inconsolable. They are cranky, tired, and any little thing can set them off. They really need to go to bed, but they are fighting sleep tooth and nail!

When a kid is having a Code 19, inconsolable for no apparent reason other than sheer exhaustion, nothing you say will win them over. You can't offer them anything to eat, because they don't want it. If you suggest their favorite toy, they'll refuse and fall out on the floor in a Code 13. They might ask for the sippy cup, then change their minds and want a snack. You'll give them a snack, and they'll scream no and run away because they wanted something different. The only thing that seems to make them happy is screaming or crying. It is a few irrational hours that finally end when they pass out from exhaustion.

The Witching Hour is the most perplexing and frustrating Code to deal with. You might even wonder if you should put the house up for sale with the kids still in it! The Witching Hour is, as Forrest Gump famously said, "Like a box of chocolates. You never know what you're going to get!" The kids may have a Code 12. They might upgrade to a Code 13. They could spread the misery onto their siblings with a Code 17. Sometimes it can be an all-out Code 57/11 (as you'll soon see in Chapter 11). Regardless, there's only one solution to a Code 19: bedtime! The following story is the perfect example.

One afternoon, I accompanied Mom and her two daughters, four-year-old Katie and seven-year-old Susan, to a four p.m. birthday party. Keep in mind that the Witching Hour starts at five p.m.!

As Katie and I were heading out to the car, Susan was having a Code 12 over a pair of shoes. She wanted to wear pink sandals, but the party had a water theme, so her water shoes were more appropriate. Susan yelled at Mom, snatched off the hat she was wearing on her head, and slammed it onto the ground, shouting, "Damn hat!"

Needless to say, she earned herself a time-out on that one! Meanwhile, back in the car, Katie, the star of our Code 19, was having her own Code 12! She couldn't buckle her harness seat belt. She had attached the top portion, but the bottom was problematic.

I asked her in a calm voice, "Katie, what's going on?"

She started scream-singing back at me, "I. Can't. Do. The. Bottom!"

I said, "No problem! I'll help you."

Katie answered back with more scream-singing. "No! I want to do it myself!"

I still moved in to help, but she swatted my hands away. There really wasn't much I could do at that point but allow her to figure it out, which she did eventually. Susan and Mom emerged from the house, fresh from the time-out, and were ready to go. The brief trip to another section of the neighborhood was filled with tension. Both girls were stewing in their feelings, so no one said a word for seven minutes. I was worried; with quiet kids in the car on the way to a party, I knew it wasn't going to end well.

When we arrived at the party, Mom parked the car near the curb. Upon exiting the vehicle, Katie upgraded to a Code 13 and picked up her scream-singing where she left off. She threw herself down on the grass and whined, "I don't want to walk up the driveway!"

"But Katie," I coaxed, "that's where the party is. Don't you want to have fun?"

No, in fact, she did not. Mom and I had to give Katie a minute to get herself together, as neither of us was able to carry her. Meanwhile, Susan had an instant change of heart about her shoes. "Oh, my goodness, there's a slip-and-slide!" she exclaimed, suddenly grateful for her water shoes. She took off running.

Katie finally gathered herself, and we made it up the driveway to the house and the enormous backyard. Now, I must tell you, this kid party was over the top! It was like a theme park back there! There was a zip line (yes, I said a zip line!), a huge trampoline, the colossal slip-and-slide, plus a spread of food you wouldn't believe. There was even a lady blowing enormous bubbles and putting the kids *inside* the bubbles!

All the kids (and a few adults) were running around screaming and having fun—well, all except Katie. Yes, she was the only four-year-old amidst a playtime wonderland whose reaction to it all was, "Meh." She only wanted to graze at the food table. Neither Mom nor I could encourage her to take part in anything! So, we gave her some space and kept an eye on her from a distance.

I looked at the time. It was past five p.m., and I knew we were out of time. The crankiness was about to get turned up to another level. It was only a matter of minutes! As the party wound down around six p.m., the party hostess came out with goodie bags. But, the favors came with a stipulation. She announced, "If you have a sibling, you can share the goodie bag."

Now, that announcement would send any *uncranky* kid over the edge. I mean, who wants a goodie bag to be community property? Moaning and groaning erupted. That was a hand-delivered invitation for those kids to violate Codes 15 and 17, with an assist by Codes 12 and 13! Basically, the party host set off all the Codes with one sentence for every child with a sibling!

Susan, being the oldest, snatched the bag before Katie could even blink. That sent Katie over the edge. At that moment, it was a point of no return. That was all she wrote. There was nothing else for Mom and me to do. Katie's distress kicked into overdrive.

As we tried to walk back down the driveway to the car, Katie just whined about *everything*! "I don't want to walk down the driveway! I didn't get enough punch! I didn't get enough snacks!" Keep in mind, she ate for two hours straight. I really couldn't blame her for her irritability, though; it was the Witching Hour talking. Back in the car, we had a repeat performance of the seatbelt ordeal. Any offers of help made her even more frustrated.

At home, things got worse. Mom told the girls to play for a little while. Katie had an outburst. Mom put dinner on the table. Katie fell out on the floor in a Code 13 because she didn't want to eat. Bath time was equally a struggle. I think Mom was just as ready for bedtime as Katie was! As soon as Katie's head hit the pillow, she was out like a light.

The whole ordeal had worn Mom out. She turned to me and asked in bewilderment, "The last few hours . . . what was that?"

That, my friends, was the Witching Hour on steroids! I wanted to tell Mom that a late-afternoon birthday party for a four-year-old who didn't have a nap was not a good idea. In fact, the whole afternoon and evening were somewhat predictable. The girls had had a full day before attending this summer party. They had woken up early that day. They had taken part in a day camp that morning. From there, they had had an early-afternoon playdate. Then, with no downtime, they attended the mini–theme park party. I mean, that was like sending a personal invitation for the

Witching Hour to show up on your doorstep! Katie was so tired, she didn't know how to express herself, so it was no wonder she was a walking Code 19 waiting to happen!

Much like Code 11, the best way to deal with a Code 19 is to do all you can to avoid it. That means children five and under should have plenty of rest. Adults must remember that kids are not used to the long, grueling hours of activities we put ourselves through. If you have young ones under five, insist that they get their midday nap. It may get harder to convince kids five years old and up to take a midday nap, but just because they protest doesn't mean they don't need it.

Be sure to manage their schedule and avoid overloading them with back-to-back activities. This goes for young and older children alike. Keep in mind that even though they might not act like a toddler, older kids can still give you their own version of a Code 19.

However, if all careful planning fails and you are tortured with two to three hours of the Witching Hour, my suggestion is to get them to bed as quickly as possible! Remember, that is the only resolution for a Code 19. And once you've survived, pour yourself a stiff shot of whiskey. You'll need it!

Chapter 10

Code 20: Bedtime Is a Solo Sport

'm starting a petition to rename "bedtime." I think we should call it "wartime." Why? Because it's often an epic tug-of-war between parents and children. Parents are eager for bedtime because it means there will finally be peace and quiet in the house. You can have a few moments to hear yourself think (and enjoy your adult sippy cup!). But kids dread bedtime like the plague! Just threaten a kid with going to bed early as a punishment, and they instantly start in with the weeping, wailing, and gnashing of teeth! Bedtime means lights out, and all activity stops. It is the worst part of their day.

I said at the beginning of this book that children don't come with an instruction manual at birth (although we wish they did). Actually, I secretly believe that before they get here, someone briefs these kids on bedtime stall tactics! Isn't it amazing how every child is born with expert sleep-fighting skills that only improve with age?

Babies try to delay the onset of sleep by crying every time you lay them down. As they get older and gain more language skills, their tactics evolve. Toddlers ask for a laundry list of stuff: a glass of water, their favorite stuffed animal, a bedtime story, or my favorite: they tell you in a sad little voice, "My stomach hurts."

I waste no time, and I answer them with, "Well, you know, the doctor says nighttime sleep is the best thing for a hurt tummy. So, it's time to go to bed!"

Sure, it's a little evil, but it's effective! I've learned that when you back up what you say with a third-party who's expertise they respect, kids stop questioning you. Just try throwing the phrases "Well, the doctor says," "The policeman says," or "God says" in front of an explanation and watch their eyes go wide with awe. You just blew past their level of comprehension, so they assume whatever you're saying must be true!

But, I digress. Older kids will hit you with deep thoughts right around bedtime. If you're not careful, you could find yourself sucked into philosophical discussions with your eleven-year-old right around the time they should be sleeping.

No matter their age or the strategies they use, the bottom line is the same. Children are skilled at stretching out their bedtime and not getting to sleep when they should—what I call a Code 20. Just when you finally close the door and walk out, you hear a little voice calling you back for something else. After several return trips, you stop responding to all their ploys. That is when they pull out their weapon of mass destruction: they start calling your name. Repeatedly. Incessantly. Nonstop!

Your kids are aware that when they cry for you, they are tugging on your heartstrings. They expect that you will eventually come running to see what is the matter with them. They will seriously begin a roll call of every adult in the house (and some who are not!) just to see who will get up and check in on them. But, you MUST resist the urge! I promise you, the moment you crack that door and call their name, you have lost the bedtime battle.

Another tactic in their arsenal that's just as powerful as the WMD is when they physically get out of bed and leave the room. Kids know they're not supposed to do it, but they also know you can't ignore them when they are standing in the middle of your bedroom, staring you in the face. The worst thing you can do is engage them in an argument and yell at them for being out of bed. Why? Because the longer you go back and forth with them, the more time out of bed they've gained.

Do you want to mess with your kid's mind? Get up and walk them back to their room without saying one word to them. They won't know what just happened! Repeat that process as many times as necessary until they tire themselves out or finally get the picture: you mean business.

I haven't shared a specific story for Code 20 because I don't think I need to. As I am describing the war zone that is bedtime, I am probably triggering plenty of flashbacks to your own battle stories! So, I'd rather spend the rest of this chapter sharing with you how to nip the stall tactics in the bud so you can emerge victorious. Remember, I go hard for Team Parents!

Let me start by saying it is challenging to eliminate every stall tactic your kids might invent. You can, however, drastically reduce stall tactics by establishing a firm bedtime routine. As soon as a baby can walk, I start them on a bedtime routine. Setting their expectations in advance is essential. I let my kids know that once we cross the threshold of the bedroom for bedtime, no one else is allowed. "Bedtime is a solo sport." Bedtime is something they need to do alone. And, once I leave the room and close the door, it is a point of no return. I don't come back into the child's room for any reason until it is time for them to get up in the morning. I firmly establish that they are not to leave for any reason unless they *see* (not *smell*) fire. Don't worry, I'll show you how I do that.

Before the point of no return, though, I make sure we have a little ritual to signal that bedtime is upon us. You can include whatever steps you'd like in your bedtime routine, just make sure you follow it consistently. For example, you might want to start with a light snack of fruit about thirty minutes before bed (so that "I'm hungry" can't be used against you later), then have them brush their teeth. Next up can be a story in bed, then prayer if you are spiritual. Finally, it is lights out.

An essential part of the bedtime routine is making sure they already have all their "peeps" together before lights out so they need not ask for them. Remember the "peeps" from Code 11? Their "peeps" are the toys or objects your child needs to feel comfortable and secure so you can turn out the lights and close the door. You never want them to say, "Where is Binky? I can't go to sleep without my rainbow unicorn!"

About an hour before bed, make sure their bunny, fluffy, Wa-Wa, Woof-Woof, favorite blanket, etc. is already in their bedroom ahead of time. Otherwise, your child WILL send you all over the house looking for that object as a way of delaying going to sleep.

You may find that you must limit the "peeps" if the request list gets too long. You don't want kids being smothered or poked by a toy while they are sleeping. If they want a lot of "peeps," maybe one soft object can be in bed with them while the others hang out on their nightstand, watching over them.

Another essential component of a successful bedtime routine is to set up the environment in their bedroom. They must be prepared to stay in it all night by themselves. As I said earlier, once

I've put a child to bed and walk out the door, it is a point of no return for me. I learned early on that the moment you cave in and go back into their room to see what new stall tactic they're trying out on you, they've already won.

You don't want kids walking out of their bedroom to wander around in the dark because they are thirsty, hungry, or scared. So, one thing to have on hand is a sippy cup (or regular cup if the child is older) of water next to the bed. Kids always seem to get super thirsty and hungry right at bedtime or in the middle of the night. Nip that tactic in the bud by being prepared.

Also, many kids don't like being in the dark by themselves, so a night-light is essential. However, I've found something that takes it a step further. Over the last few years, I've introduced several families to the stoplight alarm clock. It looks just like a traffic light. When the light is red, it means it is not okay to leave the room. As it gets closer to the set time for getting up, it will glow yellow. Finally, when the alarm goes off, the green light shines, indicating it is now okay to leave the room. This clock is my secret weapon for enforcing the point of no return. There are several versions of the clock available for purchase online. If your child likes to climb in your bed in the middle of the night or seems to have a knack for waking you up just when your sleep is getting good, you must get one of these clocks. It will change your life!

There is one final way I prepare the environment. While my kids know they cannot come out of the room until the green light says go, it doesn't adequately address what the child should do if they wake up too early and can't get back to sleep. Some kids will stay in their bed and stare off into space until they fall back asleep. But, this may not work for all kids, all the time. So, I make sure they have books and quiet toys that are easily accessible to them inside their room. This way, they can keep themselves occupied.

Whew! That was a lot of information, so let me summarize everything for you in a checklist so you can help your kids play bedtime like the solo sport it is.

1. Thirty minutes to an hour in advance, prepare the environment for bedtime.
    *   Make sure you have all their "peeps."
    *   Make sure a cup of water is easily accessible for them in their room.
    *   Make sure quiet toys or activities are

easily accessible for them in their room.

- Make sure you have your stoplight alarm clock set for the correct wake-up time.

2. Follow the elements of your bedtime routine (for example: snack, teeth-brushing, story time, prayer, lights out).
3. Stick firmly to your point of no return.
   - Try not to answer if they keep calling your name. They may fall back asleep.
   - If they leave their room, walk them back to their bed in silence.
   - Repeat as many times as necessary.

When you arm yourself with the right tools, you will have a tactical advantage for winning the bedtime battles. The key to winning the war is being consistent with your bedtime routine. When kids see your consistency, they will stop testing you.

Your best defense against stall tactics is preparation on all fronts. If bedtime has been chaotic for you, expect that it may take several days or even weeks before a child will get used to a new routine. However, the day they go down and stay down without a fuss is cause for celebration! On that evening, you can enjoy a nice, strong cognac and consider your bedtime dragon slain!

Chapter 11

Code 57/11: The S#*t Has Hit the Fan!

57/11! I have been hinting at the absolute horror that is a fiddy-seben eleven all throughout the book, and now it's finally here. This is (literally and figuratively) the Mother of All Codes, primarily because this is the first Code I created. The other reason is that the nature of a fiddy-seben eleven is as if all the other Codes are happening at once, amplified to the max! Code 57/11 is when everything that could go wrong has gone wrong. However, before I can even give you an example of a fiddy-seben eleven, I have to tell you the story of how I came up with the name.

Code 57/11 is also known as "The S#*t Has Hit the Fan" because of one little boy from early in my career as a nanny. We'll call him "Joey." At the time, I was still potty-training him. One day, he used the bathroom on his own to do a number-two. He was in the bathroom all happy-go-lucky, humming to himself. I came to the bathroom, as was my custom, to help make sure he cleaned up properly. When I opened the bathroom door, I wasn't prepared for what I saw.

Joey literally had an explosive blow-out! I don't know how he did it while remaining on the toilet, but there was poop *everywhere* in the bathroom. There was poop in the toilet. There was poop on the toilet. There was poop on the floor. There was even poop on the walls! I was frozen in horror. I did not know what to do at that moment! I finally gathered myself, closed the bathroom door, and walked out. In my stunned state, I managed to get Joey clean, but there was still a beast in the bathroom I had to deal with. My young twenty-something self wasn't prepared for that!

That situation was so horrifying that when I

got home, I drank to calm my nerves down. Seeing that fiasco did something to my soul! I didn't know *what* had happened or even what to call it! So, it got the name "fiddy-seben eleven." That incident happed back in 1998. To this day, twenty years later, I DO NOT use the same bathroom kids use, because I don't know what has happened in there. I get a "Joey flashback," and I can't do it. I am still traumatized!

So, that's how this Code got its name. Over the years, Code 57/11 became synonymous with the worst-case scenario you can imagine. For example, if a kid falls off the jungle gym and all you see is blood, that is a worst-case scenario. It can mean the worst of the worst behavior. It could be when Codes from 11 through 20 are happening all at once, then go into overdrive! A fiddy-seben eleven can also be a situation you might describe as "What the heck was THAT?" Finally, a fiddy-seben eleven can be all of the above wrapped up in a poop-colored bow!

Do I have another story that illustrates a fiddy-seben eleven? You bet I do! This one started as a Code 19 and morphed into a fiddy-seben eleven. Plus, you'll see special appearances by Code 16 and Code 17. And just for giggles, our good friends Code 12 and Code 13 will make guest appearances. Strap in, because here we go!

First, let me set the scene. Our characters are four kids, two parents, and one Drinking Nanny. The setting is a restaurant at twilight, well within the Witching Hour. The adults' mission is to get the kids in the car, get them home for a bath, read a story, and finally bedtime. That's it. Three simple things. Bath. Story. Bed.

Remember how I said this started off as a Code 19? You will recall from Chapter 9 that the Witching Hour is when the kids are inconsolable, mainly because they're exhausted and fighting sleep. It is important to note that three of the four children were under five years of age. Now that I've set the scene, let's pick up the action as the adults attempt to move the children from the restaurant into the family vehicle.

The youngest, a two-year-old, was the easiest to get into her car seat. It was the two middle children, four- and five-year-old boys, who were a challenge. This family had a full-sized SUV, and like another family I've described, there was always a fight for the coveted back-row car seat. Welcome back, Code 16, it's been a few chapters! Nobody wanted to "get in where they fit in." So, the four- and five-year-olds were bucking and arching their backs, squirming, doing just about everything to wiggle their way to the back seat. These kids were straight up fighting the adult trying to put them into car seats . . . and were winning!

Meanwhile, the oldest child, a seven-year-old boy, began harassing the two-year-old who was strapped in. She told him to stop several times, but he ignored her. So, in retaliation, she wrapped her finger around her brother's hair and yanked on it—hard! His yelps only added to the chaos in the car.

As you know, misery loves company. The seven-year-old decided that someone else needed to feel his pain. He went over to the five-year-old's seat, sat on him, and slid to the floor. Well, little brother didn't appreciate that. With his free leg, the five-year-old planted two kicks into his brother's side.

A choir of cries erupted in dissonant harmony in the car. The two-year-old girl hadn't quite gotten over being terrorized by her older brother, so she was still crying. The five-year-old was freshly angry at the seven-year-old. And the oldest child's pain had increased: his head was still hurting from having his hair pulled, and now he had tiny footprints on his side. Nothing had happened to the four-year-old boy, but he decided to "sympathy cry" because he was missing out on everyone else's pain! And because it was the Witching Hour, no adult could reduce the choir's volume or intensity the whole ride home.

Once at the house, things only got worse. Each adult literally had to drag a child from their seat into the house. The kids wouldn't settle down for anything, not even the seven-year-old! They were running through the house. Sippy cups were flying. One kid broke out into a Code 12. When that almost finished, a Code 17 broke out. Then a Code 13 popped up. They were just running through the whole list of Codes! Nothing we could offer pacified them—not a snack, not time-out threats, nothing! Every child had simultaneously lost it.

Ladies and gentlemen, welcome to a full-on fiddy-seben eleven!

Mom made the executive decision that bath time wasn't happening. Everyone needed to go straight to bed. The adults decided it was time to divide and conquer. Each adult had a child assigned to them. I started with the two-year-old because she was the easiest to get into bed (and the most likely to stay there). I doubled back for another one. The four-, five-, and seven-year-olds were each kicking, screaming, and holding on to the doorframes of their respective rooms because they didn't want to go to bed! It was a miracle we got their pajamas on. When each of them finally got into their beds, we still heard their muffled cries and hollers from behind closed doors. After fifteen minutes, the house grew silent. It was like each ran into the same brick wall and their steam puffed out. They had all finally fallen asleep.

Feeling shell-shocked, Mom and I both wandered into the kitchen. We both were looking for something strong to drink! She looked at me in wide-eyed wonderment and said, "What. Was. That?"

That was a fiddy-seben eleven! That is why sleep was the only thing that put an end to the dramatics. I do not have a magic formula or three cute steps for getting through a Code 57/11, because they don't happen often. But when they do, the only thing you can do is survive it as best you can. Just have your tequila ready for when you come through on the other side!

Afterword

The Last Drink

Whatever your favorite drink is to sip on when you want to relax, now is the time to enjoy it, because I'm done! It's after eight p.m. My feet are up, I've got a cold light beer in my hand, and I'm about to ramble off a few last thoughts.

This has been a great ride! All of my nannying experiences led to me writing this book. I've been on wild adventures and in awesome pantries! (To this day, nobody's pantry beats the Hartleys', Cottons', Greenes', Smiths', and Schaefers'!)

I am genuinely grateful for each family I've worked with and for every child I've ever cared for. It takes a lot to open your home to a stranger and trust them to take care of your children in your absence. So, I want to give a huge, public thank-you to the parents who placed their trust in me.

I am thankful for my on-the-job experiences, as

they have taught me so much. Kids have the power to change you for the better, so I'm appreciative to my families for the opportunity to "borrow" their kids so I could grow as a person.

As a nanny, I've received on-the-job training on how to get along with people in different environments and spaces. For instance, when I was on a long car trip with kids who were Code 12ing on me, then I had to stay in the same hotel room with them was an amazing lesson to learn. One of the biggest life lessons I've learned because of what I do is how to give more of myself and not be so self-centered.

Remember, I am a single woman with no biological children of my own. When I'm not working, I love to decompress with a little solitude. I spend time with my biological family and my friends on my own schedule.

When I was younger, I was kind of selfish and self-centered. When I began accompanying my families on trips, I learned compassion and how to share. Besides, every family I work with becomes part of my own extended family. So, I keep adding more people to my life to love with each assignment.

This journey has shown me how critical families are to the strength of our society. The work I do has helped me improve my relationships with my biological family and my friends. It has even helped give me the strength to share my experiences with the world by writing this book.

I love how being a nanny has changed me. As I became a better person, it made me better at what I do. I improved at my trade. I excelled at caring for children. And as a result, my business serving celebrities and high-powered business executives grew. It has been a win-win situation for me. So, to all my parents, please know how indebted I am to you.

I'd also like to take a moment and show some love to "my kids." Shout-out to all my kids I've ever cared for! Some are adults in their twenties now, but I remember you all by name. You are each unique. My prayer for you and your life is to know the sky is the limit for you! Thanks for allowing me to love you and watch you grow.

Last but not least, I have to show some love to you, my reader. Thank you so much for picking up this book with the crazy title! I know I probably had you going for a minute, but you stuck it out 'til the end. I can't thank you enough for your support.

This book you're holding in your hands is my blood, sweat, and tears. I wrote it with a lot of love. It is all the techniques I've developed over the years to help raise amazing children. I hope what I have shared helps you raise your children with equally successful (or more significant!) results.

Until next time!

About the Author

Kimberly "MeMi" Joan is a Christmas baby, born on December 25, 1969, in Little Rock, Arkansas, to educator parents. She holds a BA in history from the University of Arkansas at Pine Bluff. Destined to work with children, she started a babysitting hustle as a preteen. She launched her career by working in daycares and public schools in Atlanta. The Drinking Nanny has been a private nanny to celebrities and famous businesspeople since 2001.